D0026722

LG #	COMPOSER, TITLE	TEXT PAGE	8-CD SET	4-CD SET
24.	Bach: *Brandenburg Concerto* No. 2 in F major	209		
	First movement	209	2/27-31	
	Second movement	210	2/32	
25.	Handel: *Water Music*, Suite in D major	214		
	Allegro	214	2/1-3	—
	Alla hornpipe	215	2/4-6	1/51-53
26.	Bach: Chorale Prelude, *A Mighty Fortress Is Our God*	217	2/19-26	
27.	Bach: Prelude and Fugue in C minor, from *The Well-Tempered Clavier*, Book I	220	2/33-38	1/54-59
28.	Gay: *The Beggar's Opera*, end of Act II	227	2/52-54	—
29.	Haydn: String Quartet in D minor, Op. 76, No. 2 (*Quinten*), fourth movement	258	2/62-67	—
30.	Mozart: *Eine kleine Nachtmusik*, K. 525	264		
	First movement	264	3/48-52	1/60-64
	Second movement	265	3/53-58	1/65-70
	Third movement	266	3/59-61	1/71-73
	Fourth movement	266	3/62-67	1/74-79
31.	Mozart: Symphony No. 40 in G minor, K. 550, first movement	271	4/1-5	—
32.	Haydn: Symphony No. 94 in G major (*Surprise*), second movement	276	2/55-61	2/1-7
33.	Beethoven: Symphony No. 5 in C minor, Op. 67	284		
	First movement	285	4/32-37	2/8-13
	Second movement	286	4/38-44	2/14-20
	Third movement	287	4/45-48	2/21-24
	Fourth movement	288	4/49-56	2/25-32
34.	Mozart: Piano Concerto in G major, K. 453	291		
	First movement	291	3/11-21	2/33-43
	Second movement	292	3/22-27	—
	Third movement	293	3/28-34	—
35.	Beethoven: Violin Concerto in D major, Op. 61, third movement	295	4/24-31	—
36.	Mozart: Piano Sonata in A major, K. 331, third movement	299	3/4-10	—
37.	Beethoven: Piano Sonata in C minor, Op. 13 (*Pathétique*)	304		
	First movement	304	4/6-11	—
	Second movement	305	4/12-16	2/44-48
	Third movement	306	4/17-23	—
38.	Haydn: *The Creation*, Part I, Nos. 12-14	310	3/1-3	—
39.	Mozart: *The Marriage of Figaro*	317		
	Overture	317	3/35-39	—
	Act I, Scenes 6 and 7	318	3/40-47	2/49-56
40.	Schubert: Lied, *The Trout*	329	5/9-11	—
	Trout Quintet, fourth movement	330	5/12-18	—
41.	Schubert: *Erlking*	352	5/1-8	1/80-87

(continued on back flyleaf)